STAR REPORTER

Steve lives in Cado, and his father is editor of the *Cado Star* newspaper. But today, the *Cado Star* reporter is ill and Steve's father wants something interesting for this week's newspaper. 'Maybe you can find something for me,' he says to Steve. What can he find? What is new in Cado this week?

Steve's friend Joe says, 'There's a new girl in town! She's tall, with red hair and a nice smile . . . Her name is Marietta.'

Who is Marietta? Maybe this is Steve's story for the newspaper. But first he must meet her – and this is not so easy.

OXFORD BOOKWORMS LIBRARY

Human Interest

Star Reporter

Starter (250 headwords)

JOHN ESCOTT

Star Reporter

Illustrated by
John Erasmus

OXFORD UNIVERSITY PRESS

OXFORD
UNIVERSITY PRESS

Great Clarendon Street, Oxford OX2 6DP

Oxford University Press is a department of the University of Oxford.
It furthers the University's objective of excellence in research, scholarship,
and education by publishing worldwide in

Oxford New York

Auckland Cape Town Dar es Salaam Hong Kong Karachi
Kuala Lumpur Madrid Melbourne Mexico City Nairobi
New Delhi Shanghai Taipei Toronto

With offices in

Argentina Austria Brazil Chile Czech Republic France Greece
Guatemala Hungary Italy Japan Poland Portugal Singapore
South Korea Switzerland Thailand Turkey Ukraine Vietnam

OXFORD and OXFORD ENGLISH are registered trade marks of
Oxford University Press in the UK and in certain other countries

ISBN: 978 0 19 423417 7

Printed in China

Word count (main text): 960

For more information on the Oxford Bookworms Library, visit
www.oup.com/elt/gradedreaders

This book is printed on paper from certified and well-managed sources.

CONTENTS

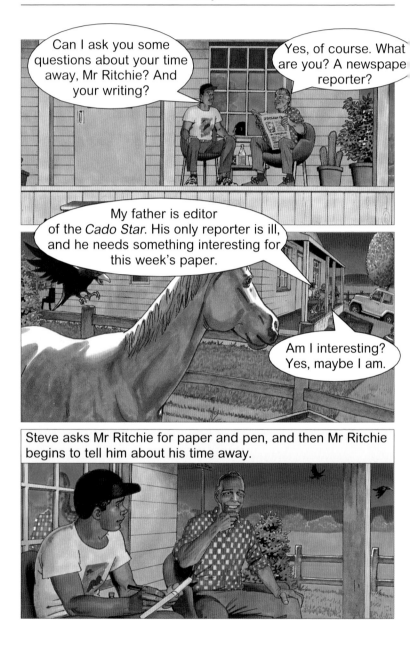

Steve asks Mr Ritchie for paper and pen, and then Mr Ritchie begins to tell him about his time away.

GLOSSARY

buy give someone money for something

camera the thing you take photographs with

dry not wet

editor an editor's work is to get a newspaper ready to read

fall suddenly come down

film the thing you put in a camera to take photographs

gas petrol; you put it in a car to make the car go

hope want something to happen again later

librarian a person who works in a library

library you can get books from a library, read them, and then take them back

maybe perhaps

newspaper paper where you can read about the things that are happening every day

reporter someone who writes for a newspaper

sell give someone something, and get money for it

shush a noise you say to make someone quiet

wet covered with water

world every country is in the world

Star Reporter

ACTIVITIES

ACTIVITIES
_____

Before Reading

1 Look at the picture on the cover of the book. Now answer these questions.

1 Where do you think the story happens?

a ☐ France.

b ☐ South Africa.

c ☐ America.

c ☐ Japan.

2 Do you think the story is about . . .

a ☐ . . . young people?

b ☐ . . . old people?

c ☐ . . . children?

2 Read the back cover of the book. Do you think the story is . . .

a ☐ . . . frightening?

b ☐ . . . sad?

c ☐ . . . happy?

ACTIVITIES

While Reading

1 Read pages 1–4, then answer these questions.

1 Who is the new girl in town?
2 What is the *Cado Star*?
3 What is Ned Reit's job?
4 Who is ill?
5 Where does Steve need to take some books?
6 What does Marietta need to get for her camera?

2 Read pages 5–8.
Are these sentences true (T) or false (F)?

	T	F
1 Steve gets wet.	☐	☐
2 Marietta takes some pictures of dogs.	☐	☐
3 The children are waiting in the bookshop.	☐	☐

3 Read pages 9–12. Who says or thinks these words?

1 'It's Cado's weekly newspaper.'
2 'There's a nice face to go with my drink!'
3 'Next time, look at your drink, Steve, not at girls!'

4 Read pages 13–16. Now answer these questions.

1 Marietta goes to the *Cado Star* offices. Who does she see there?
2 What does Marietta want to sell?

3 Who sees Marietta coming out of the newspaper offices?

4 Who has got a 1970 *Cado Star*?

5 Who is living in the old Potter house?

5 **Read pages 17–20, then answer these questions.**

Who . . .

a . . . wants to write about Bud Ritchie?

b . . . likes Paris?

Where . . .

c . . . are the 'biggest and most beautiful mountains in the world'?

d . . . is the cat?

6 **Before you read pages 21–24, can you guess what happens?**

	YES	NO
1 Marietta climbs up the tree to get the cat and falls down.	☐	☐
2 Steve falls into the water.	☐	☐
3 The cat falls into the water.	☐	☐
4 Bud Ritchie goes to work for the *Cado Star*.	☐	☐
5 Marietta takes a photograph of Steve falling from the tree.	☐	☐
6 Marietta sells a picture to the *Cado Star*.	☐	☐
7 Marietta and Steve become friends.	☐	☐

ACTIVITIES

After Reading

1 Put these ten sentences in the right order.

a ☐ Marietta gets some film for her camera at the camera shop.

b ☐ Steve goes to the café to get a drink.

c ☐ Joe phones Steve to tell him that there's a new girl in town.

d ☐ Marietta goes to see Ned Reit at the *Cado Star* offices.

e ☐ Steve gets his picture in the *Cado Star*.

f ☐ Ned Reit tells Steve, 'Ted Seymour is ill. He can't work this week.'

g ☐ Steve falls out of the tree into the water.

h ☐ Marietta takes photographs of the children in the library.

i ☐ Pattie says, 'Next time look at your drink, Steve, not at girls!'

j ☐ Steve sees Wilbur Pickett's old 1970 *Cado Star*.

2 Look at these pictures, then answer the questions.

Whose arm is this?
What happens next?

Who are these people?
What are they looking at?

What are these?
What happens next?

3 Use these words to join the sentences together.

but   of   and   because

1 Steve wants to meet Marietta. He thinks she's beautiful.
2 Ned Reit needs something interesting to put in the *Cado Star*. His reporter is ill.
3 Bud Ritchie is back in Cado. His old friend Wilbur Pickett wants to talk to him.
4 Marietta takes some pictures. Some beautiful horses.

ABOUT THE AUTHOR

John Escott worked in business before becoming a writer. He has written many books for readers of all ages, but enjoys writing crime and mystery thrillers most of all. He was born in Somerset, in the west of England, but now lives in Bournemouth, on the south coast. When he is not working, he likes looking for old books in small back-street bookshops, watching Hollywood films, and walking for miles along empty beaches.

He has written or retold more than twenty stories for the Oxford Bookworms Library. His original stories include *Girl on a Motorcycle* (Starter, Crime & Mystery), *Goodbye, Mr Hollywood* (Stage 1, Thriller & Adventure), and *Sister Love and Other Crime Stories* (Stage 1, Crime & Mystery).

OXFORD BOOKWORMS LIBRARY

Classics • Crime & Mystery • Factfiles • Fantasy & Horror
Human Interest • Playscripts • Thriller & Adventure
True Stories • World Stories

The OXFORD BOOKWORMS LIBRARY provides enjoyable reading in English, with a wide range of classic and modern fiction, non-fiction, and plays. It includes original and adapted texts in seven carefully graded language stages, which take learners from beginner to advanced level. An overview is given on the next pages.

All Stage 1 titles are available as audio recordings, as well as over eighty other titles from Starter to Stage 6. All Starters and many titles at Stages 1 to 4 are specially recommended for younger learners. Every Bookworm is illustrated, and Starters and Factfiles have full-colour illustrations.

The OXFORD BOOKWORMS LIBRARY also offers extensive support. Each book contains an introduction to the story, notes about the author, a glossary, and activities. Additional resources include tests and worksheets, and answers for these and for the activities in the books. There is advice on running a class library, using audio recordings, and the many ways of using Oxford Bookworms in reading programmes. Resource materials are available on the website <www.oup.com/elt/gradedreaders>.

The *Oxford Bookworms Collection* is a series for advanced learners. It consists of volumes of short stories by well-known authors, both classic and modern. Texts are not abridged or adapted in any way, but carefully selected to be accessible to the advanced student.

You can find details and a full list of titles in the *Oxford Bookworms Library Catalogue* and *Oxford English Language Teaching Catalogues*, and on the website <www.oup.com/elt/gradedreaders>.

THE OXFORD BOOKWORMS LIBRARY
GRADING AND SAMPLE EXTRACTS

STARTER • 250 HEADWORDS

present simple – present continuous – imperative –
can/cannot, must – *going to* (future) – simple gerunds …

Her phone is ringing – but where is it?

Sally gets out of bed and looks in her bag. No phone. She looks under the bed. No phone. Then she looks behind the door. There is her phone. Sally picks up her phone and answers it. *Sally's Phone*

STAGE 1 • 400 HEADWORDS

… past simple – coordination with *and*, *but*, *or* –
subordination with *before*, *after*, *when*, *because*, *so* …

I knew him in Persia. He was a famous builder and I worked with him there. For a time I was his friend, but not for long. When he came to Paris, I came after him – I wanted to watch him. He was a very clever, very dangerous man. *The Phantom of the Opera*

STAGE 2 • 700 HEADWORDS

… present perfect – *will* (future) – *(don't) have to, must not, could* –
comparison of adjectives – simple *if* clauses – past continuous –
tag questions – *ask/tell* + infinitive …

While I was writing these words in my diary, I decided what to do. I must try to escape. I shall try to get down the wall outside. The window is high above the ground, but I have to try. I shall take some of the gold with me – if I escape, perhaps it will be helpful later. *Dracula*

STAGE 3 • 1000 HEADWORDS

… should, may – present perfect continuous – *used to* – past perfect – causative – relative clauses – indirect statements …

Of course, it was most important that no one should see Colin, Mary, or Dickon entering the secret garden. So Colin gave orders to the gardeners that they must all keep away from that part of the garden in future. *The Secret Garden*

STAGE 4 • 1400 HEADWORDS

… past perfect continuous – passive (simple forms) – *would* conditional clauses – indirect questions – relatives with *where/when* – gerunds after prepositions/phrases …

I was glad. Now Hyde could not show his face to the world again. If he did, every honest man in London would be proud to report him to the police. *Dr Jekyll and Mr Hyde*

STAGE 5 • 1800 HEADWORDS

… future continuous – future perfect – passive (modals, continuous forms) – *would have* conditional clauses – modals + perfect infinitive …

If he had spoken Estella's name, I would have hit him. I was so angry with him, and so depressed about my future, that I could not eat the breakfast. Instead I went straight to the old house. *Great Expectations*

STAGE 6 • 2500 HEADWORDS

… passive (infinitives, gerunds) – advanced modal meanings – clauses of concession, condition

When I stepped up to the piano, I was confident. It was as if I knew that the prodigy side of me really did exist. And when I started to play, I was so caught up in how lovely I looked that I didn't worry how I would sound. *The Joy Luck Club*

BOOKWORMS · HUMAN INTEREST · STARTER

Sally's Phone

CHRISTINE LINDOP

Sally is always running – and she has her phone with her all the time: at home, on the train, at work, at lunchtime, and at the shops.

But then one afternoon suddenly she has a different phone . . . and it changes her life.

BOOKWORMS · HUMAN INTEREST · STARTER

Robin Hood

JOHN ESCOTT

'You're a brave man, but I am afraid for you,' says Lady Marian to Robin of Locksley. She is afraid because Robin does not like Prince John's new taxes and wants to do something for the poor people of Nottingham. When Prince John hears this, Robin is suddenly in danger – great danger.

BOOKWORMS · CRIME & MYSTERY · STARTER
Give us the Money
MAEVE CLARKE

'Every day is the same. Nothing exciting ever happens to me,' thinks Adam one boring Monday morning. But today is not the same. When he helps a beautiful young woman because some men want to take her bag, life gets exciting and very, very dangerous.

BOOKWORMS · FANTASY & HORROR · STARTER
Vampire Killer
PAUL SHIPTON

'I am a vampire killer . . . and now I need help,' says Professor Fletcher to Colin. Colin needs a job and he needs money but do vampires exist or is the professor crazy?

BOOKWORMS · THRILLER & ADVENTURE · STAGE 1
Goodbye, Mr Hollywood
JOHN ESCOTT

Nick Lortz is sitting outside a café in Whistler, a village in the Canadian mountains, when a stranger comes and sits next to him. She's young, pretty, and has a beautiful smile. Nick is happy to sit and talk with her.

But why does she call Nick 'Mr Hollywood'? Why does she give him a big kiss when she leaves? And who is the man at the next table – the man with short white hair?

Nick learns the answers to these questions three long days later – in a police station on Vancouver Island.

BOOKWORMS · HUMAN INTEREST · STAGE 1
Christmas in Prague
JOYCE HANNAM

In a house in Oxford three people are having breakfast – Carol, her husband Jan, and his father Josef. They are talking about Prague, because Carol wants them all to go there for Christmas.

Josef was born in Prague, but he left his home city when he was a young man. He is an old man now, and he would like to see Prague again before he dies. But he is afraid. He still remembers another Christmas in Prague, many long years ago – a Christmas that changed his life for ever . . .